Editor

Heather Douglas

Illustrator

Mark Mason

Cover Artist

Denise Bauer

Editor in Chief

Ina Massler Levin, M.A.

Creative Director

Karen J. Goldfluss, M.S. Ed.

Art Coordinator

Renée Christine Yates

Imaging

James Edward Grace

Publisher

Mary D. Smith, M.S. Ed.

Authors

Kathy Dickinson Crane M. Ed. &
Kathleen Law M. Ed.

Teacher Created Resources, Inc.

6421 Industry Way
Westminster, CA 92683
www.teachercreated.com

ISBN: 978-1-4206-3247-7

© 2010 Teacher Created Resources, Inc.
Made in U.S.A.

Table of Contents

Introduction

When writing is considered an important component of the reading process, amazing things can happen. Writing after all is the expression of things learned. It is an active process when students are allowed to discover, reflect, and create. Higher order thinking skills are awakened as students analyze, synthesize, construct meaning, and make connections through use of the written word. Research has shown that reading and writing are co-dependent and the relationship thereof is that one cannot exist to its full potential without the other; both reading and writing facilitate the other.

In order for students to optimize benefits from the writing process, effective writing strategies should be introduced and practiced. Writing strategies will allow students to expand the natural thinking process and transform that thinking into the written word.

Teaching students to carefully construct sentences can be challenging indeed. However, if a solid base of letters and words is established the task can be more easily completed. This book, *Building Writing Skills—Words to Sentences*, when used to complement an existing program, will provide opportunity for students to practice skills that are crucial when writing a well-constructed sentence. Each activity within this book meets one or more of the McREL standards/benchmarks for the area of language arts as can be found on pages 4 and 5.

Writing Standards

Each lesson in *Building Writing Skills—Words to Sentences* meets one or more of the following language arts standards, which are used with permission from McREL (Copyright 2009, McREL, Mid-continent Research for Education and Learning. Telephone: 303-337-0990. Website: *www.mcrel.org*).

Standard	Pages
Uses the general skills and strategies of the writing process.	
• Uses prewriting strategies to plan written work (e.g., discusses ideas with peers, draws pictures to generate ideas, writes key thoughts and questions, rehearses ideas, records reactions and observations)	44, 45
• Uses strategies to draft and revise written work (e.g., rereads; rearranges words, sentences, and paragraphs to improve or clarify meaning; varies sentence type; adds descriptive words and details; deletes extraneous information; incorporates suggestions from peers and teachers; sharpens the focus	20, 32-34
• Uses strategies to edit and publish written work (e.g., proofreads using a dictionary and other resources; edits for grammar, punctuation, capitalization, and spelling at a developmentally appropriate level; incorporates illustrations or photos; uses available, appropriate technology to compose and publish work; shares finished product)	46, 47
• Uses writing and other methods (e.g., using letters or phonetically spelled words, telling, dictating, making lists) to describe familiar persons, places, objects or experiences	6, 7, 10, 21, 23
• Writes in a variety of forms or genres (e.g., picture books, friendly letters, stories, poems, information pieces, invitations, personal experience narratives, messages, responses to literature)	38, 41, 42
• Writes for different purposes (e.g., to entertain, inform, learn, communicate, ideas)	39, 40

Writing Standards *(cont.)*

Standard	Pages
Uses grammatical and mechanical conventions in written compositions.	
• Uses conventions of print in writing (e.g., forms letters in print, uses upper- and lowercase letters of the alphabet, spaces words and sentences, writes from left-to-right and top-to-bottom, includes margins)	29, 43
• Uses complete sentences in written compositions	8, 30, 31
• Uses nouns in written compositions (e.g., nouns for simple objects, family members, community workers, and categories)	11, 12, 13
• Uses verbs in written compositions (e.g., verbs for a variety of situations, action words)	14, 15, 22
• Uses adjectives in written compositions (e.g., uses descriptive words)	16, 17
• Uses adverbs in written compositions (i.e., uses words that answer how, when, where, and why questions)	18, 19
• Uses conventions of spelling in written compositions (e.g., spells high frequency, commonly misspelled words from appropriate grade-level lists; spells phonetically regular words; uses letter-sound relationships; spells basic short vowel, long vowel, r-controlled, and consonant blend patterns; uses dictionary and other resources to spell words)	9, 36, 37
• Uses conventions of capitalization in written compositions (e.g., first and last names, first word of a sentence)	24, 35
• Uses conventions of punctuation in written compositions (e.g., uses periods after declarative sentences, uses questions marks after interrogative sentences, uses commas in a series of words)	25, 26, 27, 28

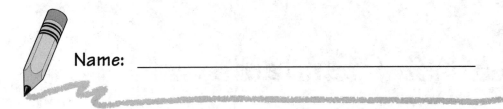 

Name: _____

I Like Sentences

Directions

Each sentence below begins with the words *I like.* What are some things that you like? Think about people, animals, colors, and food. Write the name of something that you like in each blank.

I like_____

I like_____

I like_____

I like_____

I like_____

I like_____

I like_____

I like_____

I like_____

I like_____

I like_____

I like_____

I like_____

I See Sentences

Directions

Old MacDonald had a farm. . . Complete the following sentences below to name the animals that live on a farm.

I see a _____

I see a _____

I see a _____

I see a _____

I see a _____

I see a _____

I see a _____

Name: _____

Writing Sentences

Directions

Write a complete sentence for each picture below.

Name: _____

Picture Sentences

Directions

Use words and sounds you know to write a complete sentence about each picture. Use a dictionary to check the spelling of words you don't know. Begin each sentence with a capital letter and end it with the correct punctuation mark.

Name: _____

Shopping for Dinner

Directions

Creating lists allow the writer to build better sentences. Your mom has asked you to do the grocery shopping for her and your grandma. She has offered to let you choose a few items for yourself. Use your inventiveness to create the three shopping lists.

Mom's Shopping List	My Shopping List	Grandma's Shopping List

What's For Dinner?

Directions

Use the shopping lists above to write five sentences.

1.	
2.	
3.	
4.	
5.	

Name: _____

Noun Town

Directions

A noun is a word that names a person, place or thing in a sentence. Each and every sentence must always have a noun. In the houses below list five words that name nouns for each category. *Note to Teacher: Have students keep this list for reference when completing page 12, "Once Upon a Time."*

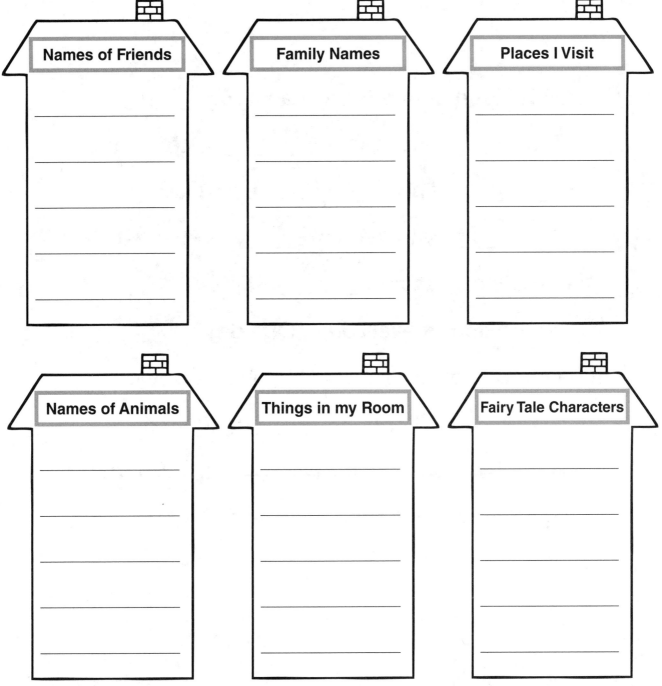

Names of Friends

Family Names

Places I Visit

Names of Animals

Things in my Room

Fairy Tale Characters

Name: _____

Once Upon a Time

Directions

Add a noun (or pronoun) to each blank below to write an original story. Remember a noun is a person, a place, or a thing. You may use the word lists you made on page 11 to help fill in blanks.

Once upon a time there was a big _____.

This _____ lived in a _____ by the name

of _____. This _____ was very large.

All _____ who lived in _____ were very

friendly except for _____ . This _____

was unkind to everyone. One day, _____

wanted to go on a walk. No one would join

_____ on the trip. _____ decided it

would be more fun to have _____. So that

is just what happened. The end.

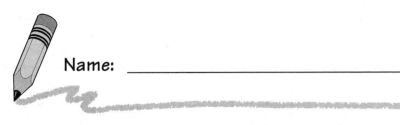

Name: _____

Zoo Day

Directions

Use the nouns in the circles below and some of your own to write a collection of seven sentences. When you are finished, circle all of the nouns used.

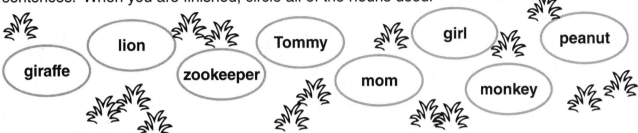

giraffe   lion   zookeeper   Tommy   mom   monkey   girl   peanut

1.

2.

3.

4.

5.

6.

7.

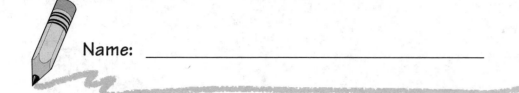

Verbs in Sentences

Directions

Read the sentence and the three words under it. Choose the verb to complete the sentence and write it on the line.

1. Can you _____ a mile?

    slowly   run   table

2. Penguins _____ in the icy water near Antarctica.

    large   bird   swim

3. Jane _____ the piano beautifully.

    plays   black   very

4. The bear _____ the hunters into the woods!

    enormous   chased   house

5. We will _____ down the mountain together.

    ski   quickly   damp

6. Did he _____ on a cactus?

    car   prickly   sit

7. She is _____ in a competition.

    great   slowly   dancing

8. My brother _____ out of the plane.

    jumped   parachute   nice

9. They _____ all night long.

    tree   sang   pretty

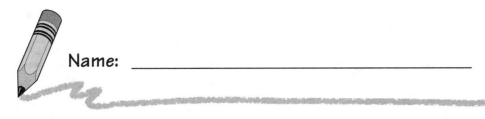

Name: _____

Writing With Verbs

Directions

A verb is a word showing action, movement, or being. Read the verb list in the box. Write six sentences; use a different verb in each sentence.

add	bake	cries	danced	explain
scared	gallop	hunt	skip	jog
kick	listen	mix	nod	obey
pour	question	roll	snores	trot
use	sing	walk	yawn	zip

Directions

Use a capital letter to begin each sentence. End each sentence with a period, question mark, or explanation point.

1. _____

2. _____

3. _____

4. _____

5. _____

6. _____

Name: _____

Can I Make it Better?

Directions

Read the sentences below. Then, rewrite each sentence and add an adjective or two to make the sentence more interesting. Circle each adjective.

---

1. My dad has a dog.

---

2. The cat is running.

---

3. I see a bird flying.

---

4. The woman drives a car.

---

5. We ate the cookies.

Name: _____

What's In The Bag?

Objective

Enhancing visualization, clarifying descriptions, and emphasizing descriptive writing by using adjectives.

Materials

Paper bags filled with objects, blank paper or story template, and a pencil for each student.

Preparation

- Purchase small bags and fill one for each player with small everyday objects.
- Create a story template.

Directions

(4-5 players)

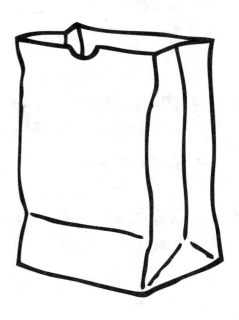

1. Pass one paper bag to each player.

2. Player A will draw an object from the bag and name the object.

3. Each player in the group will then give an adjective that further describes the object. (For example if the item named is an apple, students may add words like red, crunchy, sweet, yummy, fruit, etc.)

4. Going around the table in a clockwise manner, each player will take a turn drawing an object from his/her bag. With each turn all players will contribute a descriptive adjective.

5. After each student has completed one turn, play will now change. Player A will peek at an object from his/her bag without showing it to other players. He/she will name as many descriptive words about the object as he/she can. Then, Player A will exclaim, "Can you guess what is in my bag?" Players will then try to guess the object. Player A will then show the object. Play will continue around the table.

6. At the conclusion of play each player will be given a paper and asked to write a sentence about one of the objects in his/her bag. Students should be encouraged to use as many descriptive words as possible.

Name: _____

Adverbs in Sentences

Directions

Use an adverb to complete each sentence. Write a word from the list on the blank. Even though some words make sense in more than one sentence, use each word just one time.

1. Brook could not answer any of the difficult homework questions until she read chapter ten. Then she _____ completed her homework.

2. I want to go, _____.

3. The little girl _____ peeked around the corner.

4. I just took my _____ vacation.

5. Even though we were scared, we _____ walked past the barking dog.

6. The music boomed _____ throughout the house.

7. If we are best friends forever, I will _____ be your friend.

8. She was in a hurry so she _____ changed her clothes.

9. Instead of talking, she _____ completed her work.

10. The bees _____ buzzed around his head.

11. Even though he swerved, he _____ crashed into the tree.

12. The teacher _____ greeted the new student.

13. John is so nice. Every Saturday, he _____ carries his grandma's groceries into her house.

loudly

quickly

nearly

warmly

shyly

easily

angrily

always

too

kindly

silently

yearly

calmly

Writing with Adverbs

Directions

Adverbs modify verbs, adjectives, and other adverbs. They answer the questions *how?*, *where?*, and *in what way?*. Read the adverb list in the box. Write six sentences; use a different adverb in each sentence.

badly	daily	gladly	nearly	suddenly
almost	happily	never	swiftly	tightly
sadly	softly	bravely	quietly	lazily
safely	even	loosely	rapidly	tomorrow
wildly	more	foolishly	loudly	soon

Directions

Use a capital letter to begin each sentence. End each sentence with a period, question mark, or exclamation point.

1. _____

2. _____

3. _____

4. _____

5. _____

6. _____

Name: _____

Words in Sentences

Directions

Complete the following story by writing a word in each blank. Use the words in the box one time each.

pop	house	kittens	wish	bake	stick
stars	horse	rent	moon	Grandma's	

Grandma's House

I am going to Grandma's _____. We

are going to_____cookies. We will

also _____ popcorn. Grandma will

_____ a scary movie. Later, we will sit

outside under the full _____. We will look

at the twinkling_____. If I see a falling star,

I will make a_____.

Tomorrow, I will play with Grandma's new

_____. I will throw a _____

for her dog. I hope I get to ride her _____.

I like going to _____ house.

Name: _____

The Pair of Pears

Directions

Write the correct homophone to complete each sentence. Remember that homophones are words that sound the same but have different meanings and spellings. To give your sentence correct meaning, it is important to use correct word spelling.

1. The _____ of my school teaches us to be kind to others. (principle/ principal)

2. There are seven days in the _____. (week/ weak)

3. My favorite _____ is a reindeer named Rudolph. (dear/ deer)

4. The _____ swims in the ocean near Alaska. (wail/ whale)

5. What is that _____ ? I do not like the smell. (cent/ scent)

Write or Right

Directions

Now write six of your own using one of each homophone pair below.

(threw/ through)   (you/ ewe)   (towed/ toad)   (see, sea)   (nose/ knows)   (knot/ not)

1.	
2.	
3.	
4.	
5.	
6.	

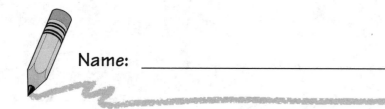

Subjects and Verbs

Directions

A complete sentence contains a subject and a verb. The subject is a noun or noun phrase that comes before the verb. It is a word or group of words that answers the questions 'who?' or 'what?' the sentence is about. The verb tells what the subject does, what is done to the subject, or the condition of the subject. In each of the following sentences, underline the subject and circle the verb. The first two sentences have been completed for you.

1. The <u>kitten</u> (purred) softly.

2. The <u>cougar</u> (chased) its prey.

3. Ballerinas dance.

4. Stars twinkle.

5. Monkeys eat bananas.

6. She baked cookies.

7. The dog barked.

8. The plane landed.

9. He played basketball.

10. Carter painted a picture.

11. The balloon floated away.

12. Fish swim in the sea.

13. Boats float in the sea.

14. I miss my grandma.

15. The princess fought the dragon.

Word Words

Directions

Choose one of the vocabulary words in the box below to best complete each sentence.

aboard	haunt
beautify	invented
cactus	journal
dresser	knight
explain	lighthouse
foolish	moccasin
gallon	

word

1. I am so thirsty I could drink a whole _____ of lemonade.

2. The _____ of the Native American has red beads.

3. Climb _____ the train, it is ready to go.

4. The princess was saved by the royal _____.

5. I read the _____ written by my grandmother.

6. I want to _____ my garden by planting flowers.

7. The scientist _____ a new automobile.

8. It would be very _____ to throw money away.

9. The ship was guided to shore by the distant _____.

10. The desert _____ was in full bloom.

11. The ghost wanted to _____ the rickety old house.

12. My _____ is full of clothes.

13. Can you _____ your actions?

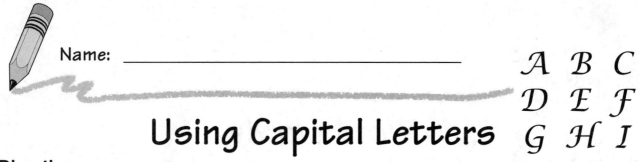

Name: _____

Using Capital Letters

Directions

A capital letter is needed at the beginning of every sentence. Rewrite each sentence using a capital letter at the beginning of the sentence. Use a capital letter to begin each name, also.

1. my friend, isabelle jones, is going shopping with me.

_____

2. i played basketball with wyatt and devin.

_____

3. are skyler and mario going bowling with kyle?

_____

Directions

Write three sentences in the box below. Begin each sentence with a capital letter. Include the name of at least one person in each sentence; use two names if you begin a sentence with someone's name.

1.	
2.	
3.	

Periods

Directions

A sentence begins with a capital letter and ends with a punctuation mark such as a period. Most importantly, it expresses a complete thought. Read each set of words. If the words make sense together by naming a complete thought, circle the number at the beginning of the sentences and place a period at the end. If part of the thought is missing and the words do not make a good sentence, cross out the number before the words. Do not add a period.

1. My mom took me to the mall

2. Shop we clothes me

3. I found a pair of shoes that I like

4. We bought a new coat for winter

5. Red it blue hood with is

6. Jeans and shirts

7. Next, we looked at backpacks

8. We hunted for backpacks in three stores

9. Perfect backpack last store

10. Before going home we shopped for school supplies

11. Glue, crayons, markers, scissors, paper, notebooks

12. My mom paid for all of the supplies on my list

13. I put supplies in my new backpack

14. Supplies took home clothes

15. I have everything I need to start school

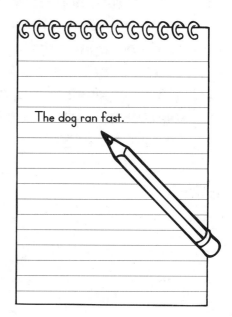

The dog ran fast.

Questions

Directions

Read the story below. Would you like to know more about the little girl? Write five questions you might ask her in the spaces provided below. *Make sure that you use the question mark at the end of each complete sentence.*

> Susie returned from the doctor wearing a sling. She was very tired and went right to bed. "Goodnight!" she said to her mom. "This has been a long day." She then turned out the light and went straight to sleep.

1.

2.

3

4.

5.

Exclamation Points

Directions

Sentences end in exclamation points to help show great emotion such as excitement, happiness, anger, or fear. Place an exclamation point after the following sentences. Then tell which feeling the sentence shows.

Sentence	Feeling
1. Today is my birthday	
2. I am so mad at him for breaking my toy	
3. I'm flying on a plane to see my grandma	
4. We saw a bear in the woods	

Directions

Write three sentences that show great feeling or emotion. End each sentence with an exclamation point.

1. _____

_____

_____

2. _____

_____

_____

3. _____

_____

_____

Name: _____

Fix It Up

Directions

Read the story below and add the correct punctuation to each sentence.

It is a great day _____ Today my mom is taking me to see the

circus _____ Do you think that I will have fun _____ I know I will

because I love to see the circus acts _____ My favorite things

to see are the clowns _____ Do you like clowns _____ They are

always funny to watch _____ I like how they drive tiny cars _____

Maybe someday I will be a clown in the circus _____ I think it

would be great fun _____

Name: _____

Scrambled Sentences

Directions

Unscramble each set of words to write complete sentences. Check your work for capital letters, punctuation, and correct spacing.

1. going trip My on is a field class.

    _____

2. mom with the went my to I mall.

    _____

3. go the Do want movies to you to?

    _____

4. new bought My car dad a.

    _____

5. We ride hot took in a air balloon a!

    _____

6. camped mountains We the in.

    _____

Name: _____

Complete Sentences

Directions

Make complete sentences by drawing a line from a noun phrase in the left column to a verb phrase in the right column. Does the sentence make sense? If not, match the noun phrase with a different verb phrase until all sentences make the best sense.

The giraffe	**paid for my trip to Disneyland.**
My dog	**caught the ball.**
The elephant	**watched a funny movie.**
The captain of the team	**chirped.**
My rich aunt	**lifted its trunk high in the air.**
I	**is my dad.**
The noisy bird	**ate the leaves from the top of the tree.**
The man in the car	**barked.**

Directions

Now, write your own complete sentences on the lines below. Include a noun or noun phrase and a verb or verb phrase in each sentence. Re-read your sentences to make sure they make sense.

1. _____

_____

2. _____

_____

3. _____

_____

4. _____

_____

Name: _____

Making Sense

Directions

Read each sentence below. Does it make sense? If the sentence is complete simply write a C on the corresponding numbered line. If the sentence is incomplete, rewrite it on the lines below as a complete sentence.

1. boy and girl walked slowly.
2. Where the mall is.
3. You are great at skateboarding!
4. Can I have.
5. My teacher nice.
6. Night is cold and windy.
7. Do you like to eat ice cream?
8. The puppets dancing fast.
9. Do trees leaves green?
10. I love to read.

1. _____

2. _____

3. _____

4. _____

5. _____

6. _____

7. _____

8. _____

9. _____

10. _____

Build a Sentence

Objective

Writing and revising sentences.

Materials

Noun phrase cards, paper, and pencils.

Preparation

Copy the noun phrase cards on pages 33 and 34 onto cardstock. Laminate for durability and cut apart.

Directions

1. Lay the noun phrase cards face down in the middle of the group.

2. Divide the group into two teams.

3. Direct all players to draw a card and write a sentence using that noun phrase.

4. Have each student read his or her sentence aloud. Award one point for each complete sentence.

5. Challenge students to improve their sentences by adding adjectives and adverbs.

6. Award one point for each added adjective or adverb.

7. Instruct students to re-read their sentences and revise them by adding descriptive words or more details.

8. Award one point for each additional descriptive word or detail.

9. Record team points and have students draw new noun phrase cards.

10. Continue playing until the allotted time is up.

Variation 1: Have team members work together to build or write sentences.

Variation 2: Have team members exchange sentences and revise each other's sentences.

Build a Sentence (cont.)

A black dog	The boy with the dog
The book	My school
My cat	The girl on the bus
The tall man	The nice woman
A brick house	The brown horse
That zebra	My funny grandma
Her grandpa	That red car
The boat	The fast plane
Her doll	The little town
The back door	The long snake
The apple tree	The gold lamp

Build a Sentence (cont.)

My brother's teacher	The pretty flower
The tall mountain	That red bike
The police	The balloon in the air
My parachute	The lion
The huge tiger	The ocean
The big fireman	Her computer
The long train	The full moon
The sun	My mom
Her dad	The shirt in the closet
Her frilly dress	My jeans
The ball	The bat

34

Name: _____

A Day at the Park

Directions

How would you like to spend a sunny day at the park? Write five sentences below using the names of friends or family and activities of interest that might happen at a park. Draw a picture to illustrate your favorite sentence. *Remember to use capital letters and punctuation correctly.*

1.	
2.	
3.	
4.	
5.	

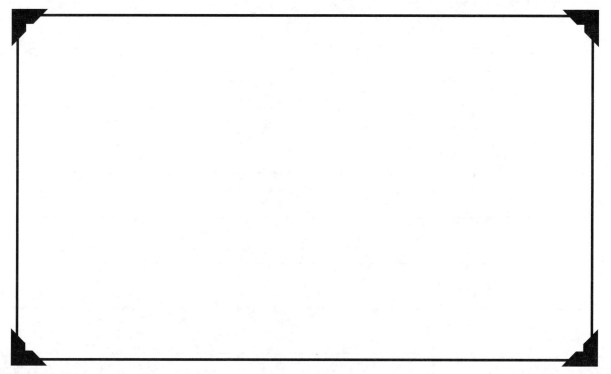

Name: _____

Spelling Words

Directions

Spell the following words correctly and then use each word to create a sentence.

_____

_____

_____

_____

_____

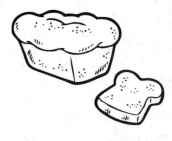

_____

1. _____

2. _____

3. _____

4. _____

5. _____

6. _____

Name: _____

The Case of the Missing Vowels

Directions

Someone has taken the vowels from the word list below! Replace the missing letters to correctly spell the words. When finished, write eight sentences using the words below.
Challenge: Can you use all of the words?

f ____ r m	h ____ r s ____	ch ____ ck ____ n
g ____ ____ s ____	l ____ m b	c ____ w
b ____ r n	r ____ b b ____ t	t ____ rk ____ ____
c ____ t	m ____ lk	f ____ nc ____
d ____ ck	sh ____ ____ p	d ____ nk ____ ____

1. _____

2. _____

3. _____

4. _____

5. _____

6. _____

7. _____

8. _____

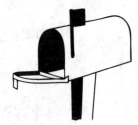

You've Got Mail

Directions

Each character below travels to the mailbox each day wishing for a letter from a friend. Choose two of the characters below and write each one a letter. *Remember that a letter needs a greeting, a middle consisting of a few informational sentences, and a closing.*

Dear _____,

_____

_____

_____

_____

_____

From, _____

Dear _____,

_____

_____

_____

_____

_____

From, _____

News Flash

Directions

Use the word list below to write several sentences on the lines to create a story for a local newspaper. Draw a picture that illustrates the story in the space provided below. Then write a sentence that describes the picture; this will become the **News Caption**. Remember to give your news story a name. Write it in the space labeled **Headline**.

horse	presents
cowboy	farmer
farm	reindeer
street	town
people	happy
Santa Claus	snow
cows	tractor

News Caption:

Headline:

How To

Directions

Think of a skill that you know how to do (such as skating, biking, swimming, cooking, singing playing an instrument, etc.). Make a list of words that are important to know if you are to be successful at that skill. Use those words to write several sentences that provide the "How to" directions for a friend to follow.

My Word List

My Picture

How To _____

1.	
2.	
3.	
4.	
5.	

Name: _____

The Party

Directions

It is party time! Your mom has given you permission to hold a party and now it is up to you to send the invitations. Below are some possible guests. Whom will you invite? Create your invitations below. *Remember to include such things as time, date, place, what the activity is, what to wear, etc.*

Name: _____

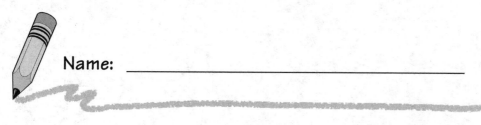

It's in a Book

Directions

Have you read a good book lately? Use five sentences to write a thank you letter to the author of the story and describe what you liked about the book's main character. Remember to use correct punctuation and capitalization for each sentence.

Dear _____ :

_____

_____

_____

_____

_____

Thank you,

_____

Name: _____

Checkpoint

Directions

Write eight sentences below describing what you like or dislike about school. Use the checklist to be sure that you are using correct sentence writing skills.

☐ Did I form letters correctly?
☐ Did I use upper- and lowercase letters correctly?
☐ Did I use correct spacing between words?
☐ Did I use correct margins?

1.	
2.	
3.	
4.	
5.	
6.	
7.	
8.	

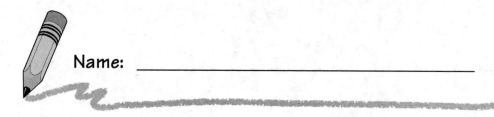

Name: _____

My Trip

Directions

Think about a trip you would like to take. Tell someone about the things you would do or see. Draw a picture of the place you would visit. Then, in the bottom box, write four or more sentences about your trip. Use your picture and discussion to help you think of what to write.

1. _____

2. _____

3. _____

4. _____

Think About It

Directions

Organizing your thoughts before you write can be very useful. What do you like about summer? Write one idea in each circle surrounding the word **summer**. Now, use those words to write several sentences in the space below.

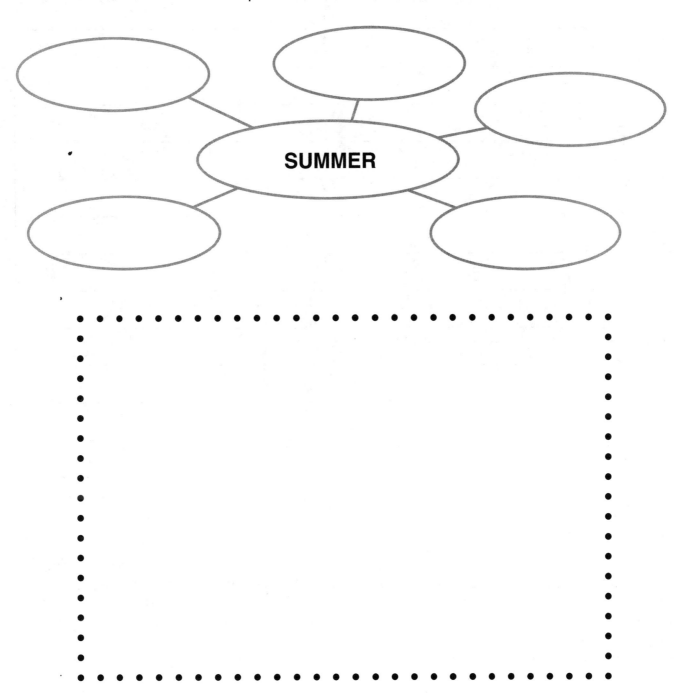

SUMMER

Name: _____

A Day at the Beach

Directions

Imagine what a day at the beach would be like. Think about what you would do at the beginning of the day, the middle of the day, and the end of the day. Write at least six sentences about a day at the beach. Then, complete the directions at the bottom of this page.

1. _____

   _____

2. _____

   _____

3. _____

   _____

4. _____

   _____

5. _____

   _____

6. _____

   _____

Directions

A story is a collection of sentences about the same subject. Read over your sentences about a day at the beach. Rewrite the sentences on another piece of paper to form a story. Put a capital at the beginning of each sentence and a punctuation mark at the end of each sentence. Draw one or more pictures to illustrate your story. Share your finished writing or story with a friend.

Name: _____

Making a Book

Directions

What activity does your family like to do together? Write seven sentences below, which create a story. Ask a friend or your teacher to edit the story, and then make the necessary corrections. Now, publish your story using the instructions below. **Note:** *One sentence will be written on each of the seven pages.*

1. _____

2. _____

3. _____

4. _____

5. _____

6. _____

7. _____

Instructions:

To make a book you will need one sheet of paper. Find the center of the page and cut in half at the midpoint. Now, fold the papers in half and place one inside the other and staple in the center to make a book. Carefully copy the words onto the pages, illustrate each, and then make a cover. You now have created your very own book. Share your story with a friend!

front of paper

cut →

7	cover
5	2

↑ fold

back of paper

cut →

1	6
3	4

↑ fold

Answer Key

Page 12

Answers will vary.

Page 14

1. run
2. swim
3. plays
4. chased
5. ski
6. sit
7. dancing
8. jumped
9. sang

Page 16

Answers will vary

Page 18

1. easily
2. too
3. shyly
4. yearly
5. calmly
6. loudly
7. always
8. quickly
9. silently
10. angrily
11. nearly
12. warmly
13. kindly

Page 20

house, bake, pop, rent, moon, stars, wish, kittens, stick, horse, Grandma's

Page 21

1. principal
2. week
3. deer
4. whale
5. scent

Page 22

The following words will be underlined: kitten, cougar, Ballerinas, Stars, Monkeys, She, dog, plane, He, Carter, balloon, Fish, Boats, I, princess.

The following words will be circled: purred, chased, dance, twinkle, eat, baked, barked, landed, played, painted, floated, swim, float, miss, fought

Page 23

1. gallon
2. moccasin
3. aboard
4. knight
5. journal
6. beautify
7. invented
8. foolish
9. lighthouse
10. cactus
11. haunt
12. dresser
13. explain

Page 24

Capitalize these words: 1. My, Isabelle Jones 2. I, Wyatt, Devin 3. Are, Skyler, Mario, Kyle

Page 25

The following sentences need a period: 1, 3, 4, 7, 8, 10, 12, 13, 15

Page 27

1. happiness
2. anger
3. excitement
4. fear

Page 28

! . ? ! . ? ! . . ! (Periods and explanation marks may vary)

Page 29

1. My class is going on a field trip.
2. I went with my mom to the mall.
3. Do you want to go to the movies?
4. My dad bought a new car.
5. We took a ride in a hot air balloon!
6. We camped in the mountains.

Page 30

The giraffe ate the leaves from the top of the tree.
My dog barked.
The elephant lifted its trunk high in the air.
The captain of the team caught the ball.
My rich aunt paid for my trip to Disneyland.
I watched a funny movie.
The noisy bird chirped.
The man in the car is my dad.

Page 31

Write a C on the following sentences: 3, 7, 10. Complete sentences may vary.

Page 36

horse, sailboat, globe, grandma, night, bread

Page 37

farm, horse, chicken, goose, lamb, cow, barn, rabbit, turkey, cat, milk, fence, duck, sheep, donkey